UNITY

Us

SOLIDARITY

US

UNITY

SOLIDARITY

Nine Ingredients to Change Our World

Delia Smith

CANONGATE

First published in Great Britain in 2026
by Canongate Books Ltd, 14 High Street, Edinburgh EH1 1TE

canongate.co.uk

1

Edited by Edmund Gould

British Library Cataloguing-in-Publication Data
A catalogue record for this book is available on request from the British Library

ISBN 978 1 83726 738 5

Typeset in Van Dijck by Palimpsest Book Production Ltd, Falkirk, Stirlingshire

Printed and bound by CPI Group (UK) Ltd, Croydon CR0 4YY
The manufacturer's authorised representative in the EU for product safety is BGC Sustainability & Compliance, 7 avenue du Général Leclerc, Paris 75014 (gpsr@baldwinglobalconsulting.com)

MIX
Paper | Supporting responsible forestry
FSC® C013604

For all NCFC supporters
with love and thanks

The human being can have no hope of an evolutionary future except in association with all the rest . . . and to not see it we would have to close our eyes.

Teilhard de Chardin

Contents

Foreword

Brian Eno

The world is changing more rapidly and unpredictably than ever before. Climate change, mass migration, institutional collapse, unregulated financial speculation and historically unique inequality all point to a chaotic, unstable future. Meanwhile, the public bodies charged with riding this torrent of change seem less functional than ever.

Governments are stymied by partisan media and powerful vested interests that pour bribe money into their election campaigns – Big Oil, Big Pharma, Big Ag, Big Coal, Big Tech – in short, Big Money. Any national government's room for manoeuvre, if it involves compromising the interests of the Bigs, is close to zero. Legislation to deal with the chaotic future is left in the hands of 'elected representatives' who in turn are 'advised' by partisan think-tanks often funded by the Bigs to produce the laws that benefit them, not the population as a whole.

'Democracy' is failing us. That isn't because it's a bad idea – it's because we've largely stopped doing it. From being a vision of popular participation, of harnessing the intelligence and creative energy of a whole population, it has devolved into a charade of pretend engagement, a form of theatre intended to reassure us that we have some control over what is being done in our names. Our participation as citizens is a once-every-few-years choice about who gets to run the government. The rest of the time, we revert to being subjects. Democracy has come to mean 'elections' rather than 'participation', a binary choice between one candidate or another.

The original vision of democracy was far more nuanced than this simplistic yes or no exercise. The vision was to harness the intellectual energy and creativity of a whole population in the process of governance. It was a vision of a creative society in which different perspectives are valued, and the constant ongoing dynamic reconciliation of those differences forms the character and resilience of the society.

Elmer Schattschneider, the political scientist, memorably wrote: 'Democracy is a political system for people who are not sure that they are right.' That is where we should start – with the humility to accept that no single individual or political party has 'The

Answer', but with the courage to believe that we can nonetheless make good lives together over and above our differences.

The important word here is 'together'. It doesn't appear very much in the neo-liberal handbook which has dominated the last few decades, and which is so much predicated on 'natural superiority', 'sovereign individuality' and a primitive and misunderstood Darwinism that sees might as right. It is this view – confounding 'winning' with 'progress' – that has dignified greed above cooperation and made possible and acceptable the absurd wealth inequalities we see now.

And yet, still somewhat beneath the surface, a new questioning is going on. Deliberative democracy is re-emerging through the gaping cracks in the old system, emerging in different forms such as participatory budgeting and citizens' assemblies. These are participation-intensive methods which invite normal people into the very centre of critical decision making – and the surprise is that 'normal people' are often much more courageous (and less constrained) in the choices they make than are professional politicians. Perhaps that shouldn't be surprising: after all, they have little to lose from change and a lot to gain.

I've followed these new experiments in governance for several decades now, expecting them to be noticed and acknowledged by the media and by the political professionals. By and large this hasn't happened – I suppose because it isn't in their interests to rock this particular boat. Or, more generously, because they still think the boat can be saved from sinking by a few technical tweaks.

As this brilliant book explains, tweaking isn't the answer. We need root and branch rethinking. We need a politics that invites people in rather than excluding them or, worse, actively demonising them. We need a politics that bases itself around long-term cooperation and sharing rather than short-term division and 'winning'. We need a politics that harnesses the natural human needs – for belonging, for creative behaviour, for self-respect, for expression and compassion – rather than weaponising them.

I must say that I hadn't expected Delia Smith – who I'd known only as a gifted cookery writer – to become a powerful voice for change in this particular conversation. But it makes so much sense that it should be she, somebody with a track-record of talking engagingly and respectfully to 'normal people', who now becomes one of the figureheads of this emerging democratic renaissance. For this is about those very same people; and about returning to them the responsibility and power they deserve. What's missing from politics is people.

Introduction

This is a book for ordinary people written by an ordinary person. That's obviously a generic term, as in truth each one of us is special. The reason I'm using the word here is to refer to the masses, the multitudes of people like me who are living on this planet, fearful of the gravity of what is happening to it, and feeling helpless to do anything. What follows is an attempt to fully grasp and face the reality of the turmoil, to investigate its causes, and most crucially to reassure people that something can be done to bring about change.

You may well be thinking, what kind of qualification does someone like me have to burst into print about such serious life issues? The answer is, none at all except perhaps the advantage of having now lived for eighty-five years, and had more time than most for thought and reflection. What age, in my case, has led me to, is far more certainty about things, and most of all a strongly held belief in the ultimate value and potential of human life on earth.

Where has that come from? I can only share with you my own life experiences and how they have eventually led me to this conclusion. I grew up in the post-war years of scarcity and rationing. Although no one had anything much, in spite of the obvious disadvantages there seemed to be much more contentment and camaraderie amongst people and neighbours. Everyone just popped into each other's houses and spent time together so much more than now. I suppose you could say I was brought up to be a people person, and living in a close community for me seemed entirely normal and natural.

My education was a disaster, culminating in failing the eleven-plus exam: so no academic qualifications when I left school. Hard to believe now, but the pinnacle of achievement then, if you were female, was to become a secretary. So my despairing parents sent me to a secretarial college. After a few months the principal rang home to advise them to remove me 'because I could never sit still long enough to be a secretary'. Next idea: perhaps I might be good with my hands. My grandfather then kindly provided the funds needed for me to enter a hairdressing apprenticeship in a smart, prestigious salon in London's Mayfair. I instantly loved it. No boring sitting still at a desk, instead working directly with clients.

Alongside a team of wonderful people whom I'll never forget, I cleaned, washed basins, swept floors and shampooed the hair of debutantes, famous models and so many really fascinating people. All the time being part of a close-knit team that seemed more like a family. What I began to be aware of in myself was how fulfilling it is to be involved in simply serving people. I was obviously good at it, as I always received the most tips.

It turned out that although I learned to cut hair, I didn't actually want to be a hairdresser. So after lots of different jobs I ended up working in a French restaurant, where at long last a vocation emerged! And with it an intense desire to learn everything I could about food and cooking. One advantage I had was that both my grandmother and mother were extremely good cooks and I was fortunate to have learned much from them.

On a wider scale, everything to do with cooking at that time was French, and whilst I'll never lose my love of classic French cooking, I began to learn about the great tradition of British cooking in the past from the eighteenth century onwards. Thanks to the British Museum, I was able to study from their amazing collection of the best of British food writers. After the Industrial Revolution, when people left the countryside to work in factories and later suffered two world wars, the handing-down of cooking skills was interrupted. Britain's tradition of rural life, fine food and the art of cooking had been lost. In the 1950s and 1960s the only way to learn to cook if you didn't have the money for expensive cookery schools was trekking out to night school.

Something I have learned about myself which has not always been very practical (but ties in with not being able to sit still for long) is that if I see something is wrong, I feel compelled to leap up and do something about it. Running out onto a football pitch when the team was losing and asking supporters to sing up was an example of what didn't work! Other attempts have similarly failed, but there's been one huge success: if Britain can't cook, someone has to teach them.

It transpired that, with the help and support of more people than I can mention here, I was able to teach the basics of cooking via newspaper columns, books and TV to a generation. What enabled me to do that for the most part was people. Ordinary people wrote to me and told me what they needed to know. When actors say it's the audience that brings out their best performances I know exactly what they mean. I became what I became, because of their response.

There was at the time much criticism of me among the upper echelons of fine dining and Haute Cuisine, from those who simply didn't understand the ordinary needs of people with no experience. I was considered to be reliable but boring. Yet why should anyone at all know how to cook if they're not shown how? It was a very simple work of service, that received what can only be described as a truly phenomenal response from a generation of people simply wanting to learn to cook. All I wanted to do was take the fear away and show them that they could. I wasn't wrong. People are always more capable than they think they are, provided someone shows them.

No surprises then now. Here I am again, desperately wanting to reach out to people who, like me, are seeing the devastation in the world and asking themselves: what can I do? What I'm absolutely certain of and am desperate to communicate here is that they can do something. The overriding ingredient that's missing from our current world is community – ordinary people simply joined together in a common unity.

Human beings are at their best when they are a community. It's just an ordinary fact of life that 'united we stand, divided we fall'. Only a united world can overcome a divided world. My mother used to remind me that something lost would often be 'staring me in the face'. In the midst of the world's turmoil, if we want to see an obvious sample of what a joined-up world community might look like, we need look no further than sport. All sport illustrates perfectly what happens when people join together with the same will and purpose. This is something I have had long experience of, having been privileged to be a football supporter for fifty-four years.

Wherever you are in the four corners of the world you will, without fail, always find football supporters. An instant association just clicks in whenever or wherever you meet another supporter. You are connected, and know you are part of a global family. True football supporters, without even trying, are all completely equal. Class doesn't enter into it. Neither does whatever country you come from, or your gender, colour, race, religion or belief. Age is also absolutely no barrier: you can be 2 or 102 and equally love going to football. You can be a lord, a prime minister, a famous film star and absolutely love being with other supporters. At matches, wherever you sit or stand, you are in close proximity to other people. Everyone talks to everyone else, people who have sat in the same seats for years, or travel on the same football coaches or trains, become a small community within the bigger one. The guy I sat next to in the 1970s still keeps in touch from Australia. I have made multiple friends across every corner of the footballing world. In spite of rivalry or competitiveness, supporters automatically relate. For me, to be in a large pub after a match packed with supporters from both sides beats any other social gathering. Whatever the result, everyone is somehow on the same page. At matches you always get the best and cleverest humour, and whatever acute pain or ecstasy you experience, it is lessened or increased when it is shared with thousands. But perhaps the greatest life lesson we can all learn from sport is hope. Nothing can wrest hope from a football supporter, however bad things are, however long it takes. There's always another game, another season. A supporter once made a joke about it: 'I can cope with all the pain, but it's the hope that gets to me.' That is what community is, and hope always multiplies when it is shared.

Imagine a joined-up world of nations where all are equal, working side by side to try to build a better future and at the same time caring for the planet's resources. Sharing all the successes, the inevitable failures, and never giving up hope. We are at present living in dark times; our world is disordered. But what we have to be reassured of, and what I truly believe, is there is no power – political power, money power, or any other power at all – that could match the ultimate power of the people joined together in unity and solidarity. Or very simply in just one word: Us.

1

A Species Comes of Age

> When I was a child I used to talk like a child and think like a child, and argue like a child, but now I am grown up and all childish ways are put behind me.
>
> Paul's First Letter to the Corinthians

I am kicking off with these famous words from two thousand years ago because I believe they are uncannily relevant at this moment in history.

The extremely grave circumstances we find ourselves in, both nationally and globally, urgently demand some mature, adult thinking. Our nation and our planet are becoming massively unhinged. Our world under its present political management is not functioning, and something quite drastic is needed to bring about change.

On your behalf I have tried here to address the situation and its causes by sharing with you the foresight and wisdom of far greater minds than my own alongside my own understanding and deep concern as to how we can find a way out.

We are being duped. Those who are supposed to be acting in our interests are not. What we now face in the long term, with the ever-increasing collapse of our life-supporting ecosystems, is mass extinction and the *terrifying possibility of there not being a human future*. This bitter truth is largely being ignored by those who have the most power to do something, and we are fast becoming what the poet W.H. Auden called 'a lost mankind'. Unless, that is, we can collectively look at the bigger picture of what is happening to us – not just nationally but universally – as our partnership with nature is seemingly under threat.

Perhaps we have forgotten, or are not fully aware, that human existence is totally dependent upon nature. Now has got to be the time for a more grown-up and responsible awareness of what human life on earth involves. We are part of a vast, mysterious universe, gifted a bountiful planet that provides all that's needed for life to evolve, flourish and progress. Surely we must all be aware that things are not meant to be as they are right now – a world of disorder and chaos, facing a spiralling climate catastrophe – and that we have a momentous challenge ahead of us? However unthinkable it might seem, if we don't soon find solutions we could well end up being responsible for our own annihilation.

Facing up to certain truths, in a world where untruth is rife, is going to have to be the first step – and much of what follows in these chapters is about that imperative. We remind ourselves that collective human civilisation, with its mastery of invention, science, tech, arts and culture, is not yet complete – and that future generations, if we survive, will have so much more to discover and achieve. Let's also never forget that alongside the horrendous violence and brokenness, there is infinite goodness and kindness. People everywhere anonymously and generously giving all they can to try to make a difference to the lives of others.

What a fully mature, emancipated humanity needs right now is to harness and connect all that goodwill and, with a united and determined mindset, stand up to the hostile forces. We have to do all we can to alleviate chronic violence and suffering, and, similarly, do everything possible to save ourselves and our beautiful world. Starting with the realisation and belief that something certainly can be done – and that each of us without exception has a *personal responsibility*.

I remember being alone aged sixteen in London's West End and losing my purse, including my money and rail ticket. My father, on the end of the phone in the suburbs, said, 'Okay – see if you can find your way home.' It was a frightening and stark introduction to grown-up responsibility, but also a parallel with the above. A timely lesson about becoming adult and being personally responsible. Looking back on that day, it contained some enlightening life lessons. Taking on responsibility can be scary, but scary or not, I found a solution. And this is the interesting part – knowing that solutions can be found is, I think, a second and maybe more important lesson. We all have to be brave enough to take on responsibility, and confident that somehow all of us together can find solutions – no matter how daunting the prospect is.

After wandering around, I found myself outside Savile Row Police Station. The policeman on the desk believed my story and generously gave me half a crown to cover my bus and train fare home. How would I pay him back, I wondered, and he suggested giving the same amount to a charity. So that was my third life lesson that day. People need people, more than we think we do, and they are often much kinder than we sometimes imagine them to be. For me, standing on my own feet, I was one step nearer to adulthood.

Translate those lessons for the entire human

species and precisely the same applies. Most of us would want to be responsible and do whatever we could to bring about change. But at present, what is patently missing on the world stage is any kind of opportunity for the people themselves to take responsibility. For you and me to become involved, to play a part in how the present or the future of life on earth pans out.

Instead, our world has largely fallen into the hands of tyrants, billionaires and the kingpins of tech, punitively filtering their malevolent idealism into pseudo-democracies without any care for the suffering and violations they inflict on our societies. Alternatives like giving political power to the people are never on the radar. Any suggestion of this is dismissed as impossible, or not pragmatic. In a world of pervasive cynicism and shallow thinking, the prospect of a shared, united world is considered naive idealism. But cynicism is superficial and does not come from deep inner thought. If thoughtful optimists, who really care, are willing to engage in what the great philosopher Kant called 'expanded thinking', they may have enough humility to at least examine *how* that might be possible.

Of course it sounds too difficult. When has anything that's supremely worthwhile not been difficult? Humans are creative, innovative beings, capable of incalculable genius on a grand scale. It therefore has to be possible to harness all that global creativity and ingenuity into just one unified objective. Namely, how to save our planet, its precious cargo of life, and make sure we secure a *safe and flourishing human future*.

The answer is, it's *more than possible*. Solutions are staring us in the face and to not see we would have to close our eyes. The coming of age for civilisation will be the mature realisation that the one and only way out of the present infantile chaos we are subjected to is for ordinary people like you and me to stand shoulder to shoulder and *join forces*. What should give us added hope is that in all this we have a significant ally. *Nature* is against chaos and disorder, and is joined in partnership with life on earth, so in the end there's going to be only one winner.

On the subject of nature, climate issues and the natural order, I want to share with you the comments of Canadian author John Vaillant, who wrote movingly about his experience of the devastation of wildfires in Canada in 2016. His prize-winning book *Fire Weather* recounts how 90,000 people lost everything they owned. And more recently, thousands more in the California wildfires of 2025. When asked in an interview how he viewed the challenge of dealing with a hotter planet,

Vaillant's reply first made the crucial and obvious point: we need to decarbonise the atmosphere as rapidly as possible. But he also said something else that was simple and straightforward:

> This is a stern invitation to reacquaint ourselves with nature and to be reminded that whatever business we're in, whatever venture we're engaged with, nature owns 51% of it, at least. And if we're going to get anywhere, if we're going to find any peace or stability, we have to renegotiate our relationship to nature. And that is a profound cultural and physical change that we need to go through, as individuals and communities.

Vaillant was speaking of what he knows is the truth. I also in a very personal way have experienced this crucial partnership. I remember years ago, when writing a series of articles entitled 'Anatomy of an Ingredient', I had the privilege of meeting various accomplished and specialist producers. What unfolded was what might be obvious to some, yet for me was a revelation. I had never fully appreciated how every precious ingredient comes to us courtesy of a very close partnership between human skills and nature.

The artisan pasta makers drying the pasta in open lofts to catch the Adriatic Sea breezes. The anchovy fishermen not knowing in advance whether the sea conditions would be just right the day I visited. (They were!) In Normandy, the great French dairy region, the farmers rely on the sea flooding the pasture and leaving behind mineral deposits which enrich the grass the cows graze on, adding a unique flavour to their famous cheeses.

Perhaps the most intricate and complex example of this collaboration comes from the winemaker. A modicum of frost on the vines kills the aphids in winter – but too much harms the vines, as does none. The sun is vital, of course, as is the positioning of the vines in relation to it. And the soil. We can only marvel at how a particular wine can only come from one particular vineyard. Only that vine, planted on that soil, can ever make that wine! The crucial partnership between sun, soil, sea, mountains and open plains, coupled with human ingenuity and expertise, is – along with so much else in our world – part of the sometimes unrecognised but awesome natural heritage of human civilisation.

Two things are required to bring about the change we need. First, we must renew our understanding of how privileged we are as a species to occupy this beautiful, extraordinary planet. And secondly, armed with that awareness, we must realise that our modern cycle of warfare, genocide and the violation and destruction of entire communities is both infantile and absurd. It's time for humankind to grow up, and to 'put childish ways behind us'.

> You may drive out nature with a pitchfork, but she will ever hurry back, to triumph in stealth over your foolish contempt.
>
> Horace, *Epistles*

2

Living a Lie

> Beauty is truth, truth beauty – that is all
> You know on earth, and all you need to know.
>
> John Keats

Truth is our ultimate human value. Without it, there can never be certainty. In a world of turmoil, where untruth seems to have become the norm, the search for truth has become far more crucial. What is the truth about the present disorder in the world? What will it take, after centuries of turbulent human existence, to bring us to a state of peace and security?

Since ancient times there have been endless wars, hostilities and violence. But right now, we feel overwhelmed by them and are in desperate need of solutions. Before we can find the cure, however, there has to be a correct diagnosis. What are the origins of conflicts over the centuries that continue to undermine the harmony and unity of civilisation? Could it be that the wellsprings of most discord come from pretty much the same source? At the top of the list is the overriding lie engulfing human existence, the false notion that humans are not all equal: racism, and what is closely aligned to it, inequality and nativist nationalism. Disguised, hidden or blatantly overt, these are the poisons that are at the root of most hostilities. Whilst humanity continues to evolve and progress, we have not yet advanced to the point of fully grasping and understanding the fundamental truth of our existence: at base, all human beings are equal. Not in what they do or achieve in their lives, because there is an obvious natural and necessary diversity in that. But in terms of something much deeper.

Each person who comes into this world is a noble and respected citizen of the vast universe that has gifted us life. Nature has provided the same blood coursing through our veins, identical hearts that beat, powered by the air we breathe and share. The idea that we are not all equal is the great lie that continues to divide and weaken societies. A lie that is so obviously against nature and the natural order of things.

A more mature assessment must force us to recognise that perpetual inequality and racism throughout the centuries is the toxic product of those who need to propagate untruth for their own interest and gain. Simply put, racism is the bullying, infantile law of the playground; in other words, 'We are better than you are. You can never be equal to us. We can take what you have because we are more powerful than you, therefore you have to do as we say.' Sadly, this childish reality is no longer confined to the playground, but has become a profound, ugly long-term characteristic of human society.

If it continues to polarise the population, unchecked, unrestrained and without due concern for climate issues, this approach is poised to eventually bring our particular civilisation to an end. Is it not vital, therefore, to address the great lie of inequality and racism and to collectively do all we can to comprehend the truth? We are surrounded on all fronts by a vast universe, the size of which we can't even begin to contemplate, and without choosing to be, we are a part of it. We occupy an indescribably beautiful planet that can provide all that's needed for life on earth to flourish. It only needs a modicum of intelligence to figure out that the truth of our existence on earth is surely not compatible with the state in which we find ourselves today – disordered, unequal, divided, adrift. The sheer destruction of life on earth we are seeing nightly on our TV news programmes has to be deemed totally unacceptable if we are to be sure of having any kind of future.

Science often uses the metaphor of the 'tree of life' to portray nature's evolutionary connection of the earth, its plants, animals and humans. For me, the piece below, written almost 100 years ago by the French scientist Pierre Teilhard de Chardin, accurately and lucidly depicts the truth of our existence. It provides one of the most illuminating and eloquent descriptions of why any form of racism is utterly contrary to nature and to the advancement of human life on earth.

> False and contrary to nature is the egocentric ideal of a future for those who have known egotistically how to reach the extremes of 'everyone for himself'. No element can move or grow unless with, and by, means of all the others as well as itself. False and contrary to nature is the racist ideal, in which the main branch taps off all the sap of the tree for itself and rises over the death of all the others. To break through to the sun, it takes nothing less than the combined growth of the whole branching structure.
>
> Teilhard de Chardin, *The Human Phenomenon*

To me, the key words are 'No element can move or grow unless with, and by, means of all the others as well as itself.'

My own conclusion, alongside others included here, is that after centuries of existence, of trial, error and progress, the horrors of the last century occurred when humanity reached its lowest point. It is those events and their aftermath, still affecting us today, that should leave us in no doubt about the change that's so vitally needed. The world's entire population was confronted head-on with what has to be close to the culmination of the great lie. The deadliest of all racist ideologies, which reared its head in the 1930s, was a pivotal moment in the history of civilisation. There are times when, as the Czech writer Václav Havel put it, 'we must sink to the bottom of our misery to understand truth'.

This was such a time. Just one word sums it up: Holocaust – the Nazis' attempt to obliterate the entire Jewish race, which had existed for thousands of years. The brutal annihilation of millions of human beings – six million Jews, and others of every race, creed and disability. Entire Jewish families, children, the elderly, herded into gas ovens to be murdered. And alongside that, other terrifying atrocities involving heinous barbarity by humans towards other humans. The Nazi project was a vile and degenerate plan, conceived to defy nature. An attempt was made to dehumanise humanity and rid the world of what racists considered to be superfluous human beings. Its aim was global conquest and total domination. It was at this moment, after thousands of years of history, that humanity came face to face with absolute, unbridled evil.

If life on earth is a learning curve, this had to be nature's warning shot. The incarnation of unfettered racism let loose on earth, and what it can lead to. All based on the same great lie that human beings are not equal. A lie that is still permeating human society – keep feeding them lies and people will eventually believe them, and confusion and powerlessness become normalised.

However, if we turn all this on its head, the obvious antidote to untruth must surely be truth itself. When all the lies are swept aside, what can never be swept aside is the truth of human goodness and kindness. Whilst the Nazis were killing millions, many more millions were connecting and reaching out to each other in their own countries and across continents. Out of the horrors of what was happening, there emerged the untold goodness, bravery and sacrifice of people everywhere: alongside those involved in the fighting, Nazi victims wrote and hid testimonies to be found and to inform us later, knowing they would not survive themselves; the brave resistance workers who saved thousands of lives; the people who hid Jews in their homes, and were prepared to risk everything.

My mother lived through the war years and, as part of the war effort, worked stitching parachutes. Later she, like many others, often lamented the loss of the spirit of connection and unity amongst the people during those terrifying years, as they joined forces to defeat a common enemy. Today's virulent racists should visit war cemeteries and observe the rows upon rows, as far as the eye can see, of those painfully young men from around the world of every race, creed and colour, who joined together and sacrificed their lives for our freedom. This is the indelible truth of humanity. What we owe to all those victims of the Nazis – to honour their memory – is for each of us to do all we can to stand up to the lie and reinstate the truth in our world. On that front I am optimistically reminded of my mother's simple but wise words: 'Give it time and the truth will out'.

On truth, I want to end with some wise and visionary words from history, from a great Russian writer who experienced extreme cruelty and tyranny himself in the last century, and whose writings and published works earned him the Nobel Prize for Literature in 1970.

The simple step of a courageous person is not to take part in the lie, not to support deceit. Let the lie come into the world, even dominate the world, but not through me . . . Once the lie has been dispersed, the nakedness of violence will be revealed in all its repulsiveness, and then violence will become decrepit, will come crashing down.

This is why I think, my friends, that we are capable of helping the world in its agonised testing hour. We must not seek excuses on the grounds that we lack weapons, we must not give ourselves over to carefree life, we must go into battle . . . *One word of truth shall outweigh the whole world.*

Alexander Solzhenitsyn, Nobel Prize speech entitled 'One Word of Truth'

3

The Wrong Politics

> We do not know what is happening to us, and that is precisely what is happening to us . . . such is the vital sensation that besets humanity in periods of historical crisis.
>
> José Ortega y Gasset, *Man and Crisis*

> We look at this over and over again [the 1930s] because it informs our current world, on a number of planes. But particularly it is a warning to us to prevent things like this from ever happening again. And we ask why was it that there were no people around who could actually prevent this terrible descent?
>
> Giles MacDonogh, *Rise of the Nazis*

The first excerpt above, written during the fascist turmoil of 1930s Spain, perfectly captures 'the vital sensation that besets humanity in periods of historical crisis'. We don't really know what is happening to us – and we *don't know* that we don't know. There is so much wisdom in those words, which perfectly explain how lies and untruth confuse and obscure stark realities.

If lessons can be learned from history, the second quote captures absolutely how, back in the 1930s, people did not know what was happening until it was too late. It is 'a warning to us to prevent things like this from ever happening again'. Those words are taken from *Rise of the Nazis*, the outstanding 2019 BBC television series which illustrated very powerfully how the German people were deceived and unaware of the scale of what was about to happen. This series is immensely relevant to what is happening in our world right now. It uses eminent historians and specialists to meticulously assess, layer by layer, the psychology of what happened to politics in Germany in the early 1930s. German society, and indeed the rest of Europe, had no idea what lay ahead.

Fast-forward almost a century later, and in his book *The Revenge of Power* the author Moisés Naím quotes Ortega's words above on his very first page. Naím then goes on to explain with astute political insight exactly what *is* happening now. Anyone who reads the book will be left in no doubt that we are undergoing a monumental crisis. Naím elaborates on Putin, Trump and an extended list of other like-minded perpetrators purveying what he frames as a malignant new form of political power. Which includes, in varying degrees, a resurgence of 1930s ideology, wars and genocide along with climate issues and Brexit, and so many other crises happening worldwide. In Naím's words, 'The times we now live in call for a bold experiment in politics.' This is the serious challenge now facing us, and is pertinent to everything that will be said here.

If *knowing* is the priority, then the first truth we must come to terms with is that Hitler's narcissistic, malevolent vision did not end with the Nazis. Something very much like it is happening in our world today. We now have not one barbarian monster but several would-be lookalikes. Whilst these modern dictators sit several notches below Hitler in the awfulness stakes, all are engaged at various levels in their own brutal ideologies, causing momentous chaos and untold human suffering.

The deadly thread running through it all is sometimes referred to as fascism. Confusingly, though, fascism has many other names. In a thesaurus, the word 'fascism' has all of sixteen synonyms: authoritarianism, totalitarianism, autocracy, dictatorship, and the rest. Arguing about what or who is a fascist is probably a waste of time. What the world is now up against is varying shades of the same lethal racist ideology.

In other words, it seems to me to be out of date to think of what currently dominates most political speak as being the extreme far-right or far-left. In reality, politics appears to have gone full circle and merged into one and the same toxic blend of tyranny. All these ideologies have one contemporary combined identity, commonly referred to as 'populism'. The term is a lie in itself, as the word indicates an approach that is *for* the people, when in truth it is quite the opposite. Moisés Naím's take on what populism actually is fits the bill perfectly: a 'strategy for gaining and wielding power'. He bases his book around what he calls the three Ps: Populism, Polarisation and Post-truth – and his list of tyrants includes political leaders around the world who conform to all three concepts.

The most alarming affirmation of the seriousness of what is now happening everywhere comes from a recent survey in *The Economist* magazine. Only an astonishing 8 per cent of the world's population currently live in what can be called a fully functioning liberal democracy, according to their research. The significance of that statistic is that most populist leaders are denying climate change, as they often receive funding and political support from the producers of fossil fuels. The choice not to listen to climate scientists is not only extremely dangerous but also deeply absurd. What is the point of power-wielding autocrats collaborating to rule a world which may, in the foreseeable future, *cease to exist*? Populist ideologies, in spite of their tyranny and power, are at base ignorant and infantile.

Twenty-first-century populism's greatest asset is a lethal weapon that Hitler's mastery of propaganda couldn't have dreamed of: lies on tap, communicated via social media platforms predominantly owned by billionaires whose algorithms serve to amplify these populist voices. Platforms that harvest data for profit and fill their users' heads with lies. The idea, of course, is that if you gather enough data about people and relentlessly deluge them with lies, people start believing them and become manipulated by untruth. *Not knowing* that they *don't know*. The deadly aim is eerily similar to the 1930s agenda: polarise, divide and brainwash people into believing lies and propaganda.

The success of this social media-fuelled populism (and the propaganda behind it) is most vividly seen in the political success of Donald Trump, whose road to power was certainly aided by Russia's tyrannical regime. Trump was, of course, the Kremlin's favoured choice when he ran for election in 2016. Russian politician Alexei Pushkov revealed the Russian government's hope that 'Trump can lead the Western locomotive right off the rails'. That was then. Now, almost ten years on, the US finds itself again living through a Trump presidency – a society polarised and divided from top to bottom. Russia's planned derailment of the Western locomotive looks to be very much on track.

Perhaps the most deadly symptom of our urgent need for a political rethink is that in the last century, almost everyone assumed that nothing like what happened then could ever happen again. We hoped, as a society, that having learned from it we would advance beyond such depravity. This false optimism has turned out to be very dangerous. It *is* all happening again, to varying degrees, and this time we are being shown all the deadly graphic details beamed into our living rooms or on various devices. As one writer, Zygmunt Bauman, surmised – every day, somewhere in the world, genocide is happening. For this reason, Naím's words about the need for a 'bold experiment in politics' are very timely – because the present day, right now, has to be a determining moment to closely question the world's political systems. How did all this chaos and disorder come about? Populism's intent to eliminate the integrity of what we call democracies, as the discussion above shows, is moving at a rapid pace.

Is it not time, then, to question *why* this is the case? Why do the world's representative governments, who are in place to serve and protect the people, seem utterly incapable of preventing what we so foolishly thought would never happen again? Whilst there are undoubtedly good, caring politicians, the systems are wrong. Our precious party systems, considered to be so sacrosanct and untouchable, are in fact powerless in the face of what is happening. They may have functioned long ago. And on both sides of the Atlantic, there have been great leaders and gifted politicians. But modern party politics is not coping with the burdens of this century. What is happening in our world is proving to be far too complex for any single political party, or even coalitions, to deal with.

The party system is an open door for populist idealism to infiltrate. Their whole purpose is to divide people and our present political parties are built on *ready-made* division. Political disagreement has long since evolved into animosity and enmity. Massive amounts of energy and money are focused on keeping the governing party in power and winning votes, whilst opposition parties expend all their energies attacking and shaming everything they do. Think about it: the whole system of government, on both sides of the Atlantic, is already so patently *divided*. It's a populist's power-wielder's dream. We cannot be surprised when they infiltrate these systems and rise to positions in Congress, in Parliament, or in the Cabinet – our outdated political systems are an open door through which populists can simply stroll into power.

America is now an openly, fiercely divided nation of blue or red. Britain was also deeply divided by blatant populist power-wielding in the diabolical Brexit scenario. Ten years of acrimonious division and disunity, non-stop dissension between political parties, politicians, families and even lifelong friendships. All of it covertly influenced by hostile foreign adversaries, just as in the 2016 US elections. If the people of the United Kingdom had been spared the lies, propaganda and manipulation, and had been accurately and truthfully informed, the outcome and its now obviously damaging and ongoing effects may have been avoided. Mission accomplished, though, for our adversaries – with the UK and the EU left divided and weakened. Job done. Another successful episode in the derailment of the Western world.

There have been many words spoken, much rhetoric, twenty-four-hour wall-to-wall news bulletins and media coverage on the failure of modern politics. There are noble theorists, experts and great minds on the case. If anything, we are bombarded with information about what's wrong in the world. Yet what is patently missing, I think, are overall *solutions*, which the political systems are unable to deliver, and so most of the world's populations remain the victims of power-wielders.

Perhaps we could rethink two extremely simple but vastly underestimated words: *common sense*. This is what a world in crisis is in most need of – a grown-up, unified common sense. And this is something political parties can never provide. There are, after all, only two objectives we should cling to – the flourishing and wellbeing of human existence, and the preservation of our beautiful planet.

If two heads are better than one, how about *eight billion*? Surely civilisation's greatest asset is civilisation itself. It is *the people* who have built the world, made it what it is, and will in the end have the final say. That's why it is they who should be determining how we move on from the present crisis. Political parties and their top-down leadership systems are failing. In a mature, grown-up world, it should be the people who, in unity with one another, make all the decisions which serve the best interests of the people – rather than just a few people at the top of the pile, dictating within the narrow limits of their own thinking, as happens today in our so-called democracies. It is so obvious that the combined expertise of all the people is bound to be more effective.

This is why the question posed by Giles MacDonogh at the start of this chapter is so crucial: 'Why was it that there were no people around who could actually prevent this terrible descent?' We are compelled to ask that question again today, as the lessons from history are there for all to see. The wrong political systems are wide open to infiltration by tyrants, who are astute at manipulating the people with their barrage of propaganda. People are encouraged to join up, belong and disregard the lies.

The reason this book exists is to ask that same crucial question, and the remaining chapters will be an attempt to find answers. As we have established, what is required is a mature, grown-up realisation that a collective society of people in unity and solidarity could become a force of power like no other. A power that squabbling political parties, media platforms or tyrannical leaders could never in their wildest dreams hope to match. In the end, there can only ever be one ultimate winner in a war against populism – and that, quite simply, is the *population* . . .

4
Lessons from History

> Never has our future been more unpredictable, never have we depended so much on political forces that cannot be trusted to follow the rules of common sense and self interest, forces that look like sheer insanity . . . Human dignity needs a new guarantee which can be found only in a new political principle, a new law on earth, whose political validity this time must comprehend the whole of humanity.
>
> Hannah Arendt,
> *The Origins of Totalitarianism*

Even a quick reading of the quote above would tell you that, quite astonishingly, it is a 100 per cent accurate description of the times we are now living through. Yet it was written three quarters of a century ago, in 1951, by a woman whose voice has echoed through history. Hannah Arendt, a German academic of high intellect and a witness to the horrors of the Third Reich. She left us with not only a testament of that traumatic moment in our history, but also a prophetic warning of how the deadly political ideology at that moment in time would have a lasting impact on the politics of the future. Her prolific legacy of books and essays not only achieves that, but contains what she believed to be the solution as above: 'a new political principle, a new law on earth that must comprehend *the whole of humanity*'.

At this very concerning juncture in our history, can we not ask ourselves why we would not want to explore the wisdom of history and be prepared to engage in listening to those who lived in the past and on whose shoulders we stand in our mission to advance and progress?

Hannah's seminal work, *The Origins of Totalitarianism*, is over 600 pages long, and not easy reading. But so urgent are the times and so important is her contribution that, thankfully, American academic Richard J. Bernstein has recently written a small paperback of only 124 pages with an urgent and very appealing title: *Why Read Hannah Arendt Now?* In it he has skilfully managed to capture the true essence of her entire work, and for me it is a must-read for anyone in despair about what is now happening in our political systems; he emphatically answers the question posed in the title.

The events of the 1930s brought forth many voices of warning and foreboding from Orwell onwards, and it's understandable that we might not want to listen, or to remember. Yet what happened to human civilisation at that crucial time in our history is still *very much affecting us today*. Surely a mature, thinking humanity in these dark and dangerous times needs not just to listen to wise voices from history but also to attempt to *take action*. To begin something new and radical, something completely fresh and invigorating. We have encountered the very extremes of evil and its attempt to dehumanise society. Is it not time now to re-humanise? To be informed by other generations on whose shoulders we stand, and whose wisdom can help us to escape our blind indifference and open our eyes to our own human potential and possibilities? Why not collectively put all our effort into what might await us in the untried, unknown phenomenon of what a 'whole' united humanity might be capable of?

Hannah Arendt's conclusion on all this was not something completely new – she had studied the ancient Greeks. For her a thriving society should subscribe to Aristotle's view that 'inequality brings instability'. Aristotle also noted that 'humans by nature are political animals' and for Arendt there was no doubting. Politics has to come from the people, because for her *people are politics*.

Another period of great historical significance for Arendt was the American Revolution, which she analysed deeply in an essay, which later became a book, *On Revolution*. Within it, she examines the revolutionary tradition and what she called its 'lost treasure' – an unawakened, *communal spirit* that only surfaces when people unite together with a common purpose. Her definition of the word 'revolution' was that it was not always about rebellion, but more accurately about change: radical change. It was this communal spirit that awakened energy, ambition, courage and daring. What we learned from the great American Revolution was the exact enactment of that. It was the people themselves who fought in unison for change and, after several years, secured their liberation. Yet Arendt was also quite certain that at the same time, within the founding of the constitution and the new republic of the United States, something precious within that struggle had been lost.

What informed and underlined her own certainty and thinking was another colossal voice from history, Thomas Jefferson. Towards the end of his life he saw a worrying flaw in the forming of the new republic. Previously, the American population was made up of townships or wards, where small communities acted together in 'expressing, discussing, deciding, and self governing'. In other words the people themselves were the politics. Come the revolution, these little republics simply joined forces. Jefferson described what they achieved as 'the vigour given to the revolution being due to the little republics who had thrown the entire nation into energetic action . . . and that there was not an individual in their states whose body was not thrown with all its momentum into action'. It was the loss of this phenomenon of people-power, observed first-hand by Jefferson, that became the 'lost treasure' in Arendt's essay. Once the constitution was in place, those who took charge from then on would act on *behalf* of the people, but not in union *with* them.

Jefferson regretted that the new constitution made no allowances for the ordinary people to be involved as before. In the future, there would be only *representatives* of the people, acting on their behalf. He felt that somehow, without the participation of the small townships and wards, the people would *lose* the communal revolutionary spirit which had played such a crucial part in securing their freedom. What the new system had failed to create were political institutions where this freedom and participation could continue to be exercised by future generations. This was Jefferson's '*most* cherished idea'; his fear was that with the constitution as it stood, a tyranny could rise in the future and that 'the representative organs could become corrupt and perverted'. What an amazing insight that was! All of 250 years ago, yet an accurate mirror image of what we are seeing in politics today.

Another voice in history, from a completely different angle and another of my own personal heroes, is a Russian scientist and geographer called Peter Kropotkin. In 1902 he wrote a book called *Mutual Aid: A Factor in Evolution*, which was described by anthropologist Ashley Montagu as 'one of the world's great books'. Kropotkin was a huge admirer of Charles Darwin, but he thought that some of Darwin's later devotees had distorted his theories somewhat. At the age of twenty he set out, beginning in eastern Siberia and northern Manchuria, to discover for himself what he suspected. Which was that whilst the fight for survival in animal life involves combat and the survival of the fittest, what 'passed before my very eyes' was that it was 'mutual aid and mutual support amongst animals, insects and humans that played the leading role in the maintenance of the life of each species, and what furthered its evolution'.

Early in the book, Kropotkin refers to a conversation that inspired him between two prominent figures – Johann Eckermann, a writer and ornithologist, and the great literary giant, Johann von Goethe. Two fledging wrens had escaped Eckermann and he recalled them being in a robin's nest the next day, the robin parents feeding them as if they were their own chicks. Goethe reacted excitedly, 'If it be true that this feeding of a stranger goes through all of nature, as something of the character of a general law – then many an enigma would be solved.' A natural support system running through all of life has huge implications, and in my own opinion it is this mostly hidden natural mutual support that, when fully understood, can overcome disorder and dissension. Moving on to studying the human species around the world, Kropotkin closely observes that whilst life is a continued struggle through combat and competition, co-operation has played a significantly greater part in the survival of all species and of humans. In his words:

> Nothing . . . can weed out the feeling of mutual solidarity, deeply lodged in humanity's understanding and heart . . . and the perception

> of oneness with each human being . . . In its wider extension, even in the present time, we also see the best guarantee of a still loftier evolution of our race.

Perhaps most enlightening are Kropotkin's studies of medieval society in Britain. In his chapter called 'Mutual aid in the medieval city', Kropotkin claims that for over four centuries:

> . . . we can speak of the medieval city as of a well defined phase of civilisation . . . with its small communities, guilds and sub-towns around the mother city . . . not placed under the control of state functionaries . . . it was a body of citizens with given trades . . . the more we learn about the medieval city the more we are convinced that at no time has labour enjoyed such prosperity and such respect as when city life stood at its highest.

And my own favourite line: 'Not only were many aspirations of our modern radicals already realised in the Middle Ages, but much of what is described now as utopian was accepted then as matter of fact.'

Kropotkin's book absolutely defines mutual aid within everything that lives. Nothing can change the truth of that observation, whatever the size of the population. He saw 'with his own eyes' what mutual aid can achieve.

In the continuing struggle in the times we are now living through, the experience and wisdom of others in history have much to teach us and give us hope. Bernstein picks out a most inspiring quote from Hannah Arendt in his book: ' "Today, when there is so much suspicion of politicians, it is difficult to resist becoming cynical about any and all forms of politics." Arendt did not believe in blueprints for political action. But she did believe, like the pearl-diver in Shakespeare's *The Tempest*, that one can recover pearls and corals from the ruins and fragments of the past that might shed illumination on what politics once was – and might still become.'

5

Democracy: A Lost Treasure

> Yet I cannot too often repeat that it [democracy] is a word the real gist of which still sleeps, quite unawakened . . . It is a great word, whose history, I suppose, remains unwritten, because that history has yet to be enacted.
>
> Walt Whitman, *Democratic Vistas*

Walt Whitman perceives the truth and beauty of democracy, the 'great word', but laments its absence as the real gist of its meaning remains unawakened. Yet he gives us hope, because whilst its history remains unwritten – it has *yet to be enacted*. I marvel at poets like Keats (see page 19) and Whitman who can articulate such profound universal truth in so few words. Democracy, when we finally identify and accept its true meaning, will prove to be one of nature's most treasured gifts to humanity – and has never had more relevance.

What are its secrets? Could it provide answers as we continue our struggle to live in a dysfunctional world? If, as is often said, an ending can indicate a new beginning, what decisively and irrevocably *must* come to an end is the distortion of the true meaning of democracy. Strangely, it's both the most undervalued and overused word in politics, a blanket term for any political system that is not overtly autocratic. Sometimes even power-wielding, authoritarian governments take licence with the word. Witness the 'Democratic People's Republic of Korea' (the official name for North Korea)! A hideous regime that's about as far away from true democracy as possible.

The hidden secret of the word 'democracy' is that, contrary to what the word suggests, it does not entail real empowerment of the people. The truth is that, yes, the people have a degree of influence – but simply having the right to vote every four or five years is surely not true empowerment. If you don't like the party, or the leader, you have the 'power' to wait and vote for another one. That is the limit of any kind of personal involvement in how today's political systems work.

The bewildering thing is how politicians are able to speak so passionately about it, fighting for our democracies, protecting our democracies, and even sometimes warning us that our democracies are under threat. It's a totally false interpretation which is now unthinkingly accepted everywhere. If you don't live under authoritarian rule then you live in a democracy. If I question that as not being the truth, I am told that what I need to understand is that the *modern* term for democracy actually means *representative* democracy. Which is in fact quite comical, as each word contradicts the other. True democracy, as we shall soon see, has to involve the *people* – and representatives of the people are not the people. If I vote for a political party who gets to govern, then yes, they are representing me – but I am never in any way going to have any say in anything they do. I can write to my representatives, and maybe get to speak to them, if I'm lucky, but any sort of contribution to decision-making is not on the radar.

If given that chance, what I would dearly like to have a say in might be, for example, my own 'representative' government's decision to allow two new airport runways and a third extension to be built. Why? They enthusiastically claim it will accommodate thousands more flights. That means pumping out thousands more emissions to join the rest of the poison that is threatening life on our planet. You wonder if they've actually heard how the effects of climate change are now happening much quicker than originally thought, or how its consequences – the ever-increasing wildfires, floods, storms, hurricanes and massive landslides – are causing thousands to lose their lives and thousands more their homes.

Go to your thesaurus or your dictionary and there it is, in black and white: democracy in our present world means representative government. Okay, if that's what we call it. But the word 'democracy' as it's currently used is a sham – what one writer, James C. Scott, describes as a 'charade zone' and even more strongly 'a cruel hoax'. Most political parties who claim to be democratic *are not*. Current 'representative governments' are not in any way making inroads into solving the turmoil in our world, and certainly not coming near to adequately addressing climate issues.

The origins of democracy, like so much else, lie with the ancient Greeks, the founders of Western civilisation. In Athens, way back in the fourth century BC, the people were suffering from a similar political crisis to the one we face now – led by a crop of tyrannical and corrupt leaders, some of them thinking they were gods (just as now). The Athenians, accomplished thinkers and deliberators, formulated a simple idea that turned out to be pure genius. The only way to see off tyrannical regimes would be not to have representative leaders, but to engage *all* the people – or rather, those in society who wanted to take part in political debate and decisions.

That meant transferring all political power to the Athenian citizens. There would be no privileged positions pertaining to wealth, birthright, money or fame. Instead, all citizens except women and slaves (unfortunately this is where their ancient progressiveness stops short) would have *equal* opportunity, if they so wished. This meant the chance to engage in public debate, to be able to speak and, most importantly, to be heard. The new political system was defined in one simple Greek word of two parts – *demos*, meaning 'people', and *kratia*, meaning 'rule' or 'power'. Demokratia: *the power of the people to rule.* As opposed to Autokratia: *absolute power* – with no citizens.

A short but lucid description of how it worked at the time appears in Professor James Miller's brilliant book, *Can Democracy Work*? This is how he describes it:

> What Athens did have was community in which every citizen was expected to participate directly in the political life of the city – and far more actively than in any known modern democracy. At the height of democracy in Athens, in the mid-fourth century BC, an assembly of citizens, open to all, met at least forty times a year. All political offices were held by ordinary citizens, selected by lot, and all legal judgements in the city's courts were reached by large juries of ordinary citizens similarly selected. And all this happened in a comparatively large commercial city that dominated the eastern Mediterranean world for two centuries.

The Athenian solution may have sounded at the time as unlikely as it does now. But there is no doubting it happened: ordinary people of all persuasions, backgrounds and class, selected by lot, came together in unity, to deliberate, not without fierce diversity, but acting together in order to reach a unified agreement. The result? An extremely powerful and effective political force, which makes a mockery of how we now use the word. Again – when, or where, in all our so-called democracies, do ordinary people have *any* sort of say or power?

Surely the indelible meaning of the 'great word' demokratia has to be rescued from the distorted sham it has become.

The stock reaction to this might be to point out that there were not so many people then, and that modern society is more diverse. Point taken – but what we need to continue to extract from the original is its essence: *involvement of the people themselves*. Adapting to a true democracy may help us to succeed in the whole business of human existence – in other words, the human project we all happen to be invested in and responsible for. Dare we mention words like peace and harmony, which surely have to be a part of what in the end we are all striving for?

The challenge before us is that the vague nod to democracy which involves people putting crosses on bits of paper every few years is no longer fit for purpose in the modern world. So, let's not write off *true democracy*, which, unlike the size of the population, has not changed since the Athenians. Instead, can we be open-minded enough to investigate how to incorporate its essence into a new system of people's politics? A system which eventually must replace top-down elitist government systems that are failing to finding solutions. Who at present among us, confined to the wasteland of the politically homeless, would not want to exchange the same tired overload of worn-out rhetoric for something new? We must all be longing for *change*. Something novel, something fresh, something within all of us that, as Whitman reminds us, has been sleeping for centuries.

We are brainwashed into thinking our lives are too complex, our world too diverse, but we are stuck in a mire of untruth. We can choose to carry on discussing how bad things are, or alternatively roll up our sleeves, take action and do whatever we can to get out of the mire. There are obviously people who don't want to be involved in politics. Yet there are others who do, and are longing to see a way out of the tragedy of what is happening, and would want to do all they can to secure a safe future.

Something needs to happen, and soon. We are in a crisis. This is not doom-mongering which accepts defeat and doesn't see a way out. Instead it's a wake-up call of the highest order. A lesson in how to comprehend what is our truest human nature. It's not a time to be clever – it's a time to be humble, and to be open to *considering* change. Cautious optimism costs nothing.

Since the Greeks are right about most things, Aristotle can have the last word here as I am more than sure he knew the truth: 'If liberty and equality as is thought by some are chiefly to be found in democracy, they will be best attained when all the people alike share in the government to the utmost.'

6

A Way Out for the World

> The different branches of science combine to demonstrate that the universe in its entirety must be regarded as one gigantic process of becoming. Which can be properly called a genesis or evolution or a cosmogenesis . . . becoming more truly human – Nietzsche's view that man is unfinished and must be completed.
>
> Julian Huxley

Sir Julian Huxley's scientific perception of humanity's future is comfortingly optimistic. He saw humanity and all life on earth as part of a prolonged universal process of *becoming*, which for me imparts enormous hope. Obviously, the fact that we exist as a species has to be part of some ongoing universal narrative – one that, as Nietzsche points out, is not yet finished. This is evidenced within humanity's long history of trial, error and struggle.

Yet all the time we see movement. Evolution happens. Without choosing to be, we find ourselves on part of a continuing journey from infancy to maturity stretching over incalculable aeons of time – centuries of learning, of groping, feeling our way towards some kind of fulfilment. Considering the awesome achievements in science, engineering, medicine, arts, culture and so much more, what has been affirmed throughout is how there are no limits to human creativity and ingenuity. Yet in contrast to all of this positivity and in the knowledge that all is not well, surely some kind of movement or change of direction has to be on the cards.

And so it is! On reaching the twenty-first century, we may have arrived at what could be a seminal moment. Optimistically, there are glimmers of light on the horizon. Something is awakening, still in its early stages yet beginning to take shape, which, given time, may be something that could influence the direction of our future.

It seems logical that since all else is spectacularly failing, what could be staring us in the face is this: in the end, it will all come down to *us*. You and me. Ordinary, everyday members of human society, along with another eight billion or so precious humans who, just like us, are learning that the future of humanity could be at risk. What we have as yet failed to realise, since so much appears to be in the hands of populist power-wielders, is that actually there is only one real power on earth – and that is the power that would exist if human beings were to seriously *join forces*. Remember *demo-kratia*, the power of the people to rule. One planet, one human species in unity and solidarity, co-operating and becoming globally interdependent. A grown-up, mature world of people finally understanding that it is they themselves who are in charge of the future. Since time began, we should have known. The one thing we cannot deny and know for certain is that all forms of life without exception are already inherently joined together with one mission and one objective: *to survive*.

If optimistic Huxley is right – and I am quite certain he is – then right now, we are seeing evidence of hints of movement and what could be a genesis, a change in the way we view politics. And potentially the key to all this is based on precisely the same ancient concept of democracy outlined above. That concept is '**citizens' assemblies**', which are beginning to engage in deliberative democracy.

This so ancient, yet so contemporary idea is now being enacted in many countries around the world (see the link on page 109) via the citizens' assemblies. There is no centralised authority or leadership – everything is organised by administrators. People from different demographic areas are selected by lot (another solution from the classical world, called 'sortition') then invited to join with others, also randomly chosen, to attend a citizens' assembly. They then deliberate on a given political subject, say the refugee crisis, or climate change, or any issue of concern to the public. The deliberators are first informed of the context by a diversity of expert speakers, then invited to do their own research, given material to study and become informed.

Next, the important bit: they deliberate together, share their ideas and conclusions, listen to the conclusions of others, sometimes vehemently disagreeing or not and often completely changing their minds on what they originally thought. Everyone is free to be who they are, express what they think, and most importantly of all, everyone is totally and absolutely *equal*. The assemblies can deliberate on a particular subject over several evenings, weekends or perhaps one day of each weekend. The invitations are again strictly by lot, so there is no option to bring a friend or family member. The names are randomly picked from electoral rolls and other demographic sources. It could mean that if a nation decided to buy into true democracy, it could over time make an invitation to every interested citizen at some stage to take part in an assembly, which they would be free to accept or not. This could also be devolved into local areas with their representatives also drawn by lot joining national assemblies. This is all in its formative stages and is not yet fully embedded as a political system, but it could be the seed bed of a new people's politics.

If it all sounds unlikely, begin by thinking about jury service. People are selected from an entire nation in precisely the same way, randomly, and then invited to listen to the evidence, become informed, deliberate together and make a shared decision as a group. Since way back in the twelfth century we in the UK have been entrusting random members of the public with the power to make momentous decisions that seriously affect people's lives. Citizens' assemblies operate in precisely the same way. The administrators sum up the conclusions, but it is the whole assembly of citizens who actually make the pivotal recommendations.

If juries of ordinary, randomly selected people can be trusted to reach the right conclusions, it's obvious that assemblies can be trusted too. Imagine a hundred assemblies spread throughout the country deliberating on a particular subject – for example, the continuing debate about restricting social media use. Where should we put the solar panels we need – in fields, or on rooftops? What should we do about the lack of affordable housing? And so on. The informed conclusions could be shared with the entire population and a vote would be cast. Wouldn't it then be fascinating to actually discover what the people want as a nation when they are first of all correctly informed and not vulnerable to manipulation and lies.

Not surprisingly, governments and party politicians are not keen on such a system as it completely shifts their power to the people (as it should). Also, unsurprisingly, the idea of citizens' assemblies often prompts dismissive criticism and cynicism. Or it sparks patronising suggestions as to how assemblies *might* be allowed to make a contribution to government, in which case there's absolutely no point. What is key is that the assemblies, whilst continuously learning and developing, are also discovering and proving that all people – whatever their qualifications, background or belief – have, without exception, a role to play and something to offer the rest of society. Because, just as Hannah Arendt so correctly stated, *people are politics*. Attendees of the assemblies that are already convening around the world are also realising what was outlined in the last essay – namely, that people in union with one another are discovering themselves and who they truly are, and at the same time discovering who others truly are. You can find links on page 109 to short film clips of attendees' reactions if you want to see this for yourself.

Citizens' assemblies are growing around the world and the country leading the way at present is the Republic of Ireland. The following example says absolutely everything about what assemblies are and what they can achieve. The abortion law, which the Irish government had failed to resolve over twenty-five years, was deliberated by a randomly selected citizens' assembly of 100 people, spread across gender, age, social class and region. Over several months the assembly engaged on certain agreed days, and were informed by various speakers, witnesses and experts from all sides of the debate – including those who had been personally affected by the law as it stood. This very emotive subject was considered in an informed debate, tackling the issues from all angles.

And so, the findings of the *people* on behalf of the *people* were then presented to the rest of the people and a vote decided by a majority of 64 per cent. That result *changed the constitution.* No politicians were involved. The Irish government has to be commended for having confidence in the democratic will of the people. Since then, more Irish assemblies have deliberated on issues such as the challenges and opportunities presented by the country's ageing population, tackling climate change and drug control (see page 109 for the link). Each assembly invites the public at large, if they wish, to send in their own submissions ahead of the assembly day.

Experiments with assemblies are now taking place in many countries. We have even seen a global assembly on climate change. And there is a film in production based on that and the assembly movement, called very aptly 'One World or None'. Another telling example is in the famous oil and gas state of Texas in the US. An assembly-style process was held to deliberate on the contentious subject of renewables versus fossil fuels, with debate between environmentalists and the energy industry. It produced a shock result, as many changed their views. The results of the assemblies have contributed to Texas, formerly ranked as the forty-ninth state in renewable energy production, now moving up to number one!

What our world, our lives, and our future are in dire need of at this critical time is to begin to learn how to live a more shared democratic existence. The assemblies are a huge step towards this. They are leading the way, showing us how effective we can be as a society when individual citizens – empowered, informed and equal among their peers – can deliberate, debate and find a way forward together, in unity.

7

Who We Really Are

> Tyrannical regimes arose at different times and places in the Europe of the twentieth century, but memoirs of their victims all share a single tender moment . . . people who were living in fear of repression remembered how their neighbors treated them. A smile, a handshake, or a word of greeting – banal gestures in a normal situation – took on great significance.
>
> Timothy Snyder, *On Tyranny: Twenty Lessons from the Twentieth Century*

Timothy Snyder is without doubt one of the great thinkers of our time. An American professor of history at Yale, now at the University of Toronto, he has written some very penetrating, prize-winning books about the twentieth century and its legacy for the times we are now living through. *Twenty Lessons* is a book everyone should read. You can read it in a small paperback or a beautifully illustrated edition with artist Nora Krug, which I particularly love. It is a disturbing book, inevitably, yet there is so much we can learn from each of those insightful twenty lessons, particularly something that really cuts through in our current crisis: *a call for action.* Action that all of us can engage in, such as extending those 'banal gestures' and naturally relating more to the people around us.

Tyranny aims to dehumanise, divide and isolate people from each other, violating our true human identity. Under tyrannical rule, lies, fear and brutality paralyse the truth of human existence, in which tenderness, empathy and affinity become – not lost, but insulated in fear and isolation. Obviously, that usually isn't the case with close friends and family, but rather in the wider general sense of contact with fellow citizens. There is now an increasing sense of division and separation between people, causing an increase in loneliness, a sense of not belonging, and a higher proportion of suicides (all borne out by the data). This is what polarisation and power-wielding achieve as their toxicity spreads and drip-feeds into divisive political systems. People feel alienated, cut off from any sense of responsibility, not able to be included or to make a contribution. But all the while remains within us some deep comprehension that this is not how life is meant to be.

This chapter's title – 'Who We Really Are' – is something I previously researched for a book a few years ago. In my research I came across one of our most lauded psychologists, a figure to whom others still refer. Abraham Maslow was an American, voted by *Esquire* magazine as the most influential person in his country during the first half of the last century. At a young age, Maslow watched a military parade and was moved to tears by the horrors of the Second World War. He vowed to spend his life trying to understand why humans fight wars and to try to establish who and what they really are.

His research was not with data or in a laboratory, but instead consisted of interviews with many thousands of people, person to person. If applied today, the results could be world-changing. At the very core of what he discovered, Maslow was able to affirm that each human life, without exception, has unique personal value and potential. Too often, this is ultimately undermined by varying circumstances that suppress our true nature. So we are pawns moved by others, rather than self-determining individuals. When people are deprived of their individual agency, not valued, and always have their minds made up for them, they become weakened. If a person's unique and true identity is suppressed, so are their gifts and potential, for which they then have no outlets.

In that sense, the person never truly becomes who and what they really are. The mental side-effects might include apathy, amorality, hopelessness and cynicism. The implications of how this affects human lives on the world-scale are truly momentous. Suppressed people, living only half-lives. Left out of the game entirely, and never becoming self-determining citizens sharing responsibility and making a contribution. Maslow also concluded that what people were most hungry for were values, principles and moral codes. What he concluded from all his research was that if children could learn from an early age about who they really are, and could become what he called self-actualised or self-fulfilled; and if they could learn, in his most memorable words, that 'There is greatness in each one of us', and learn how to live within a framework of shared human values, then this, surely, 'could lead to a new kind of civilisation'.

Perhaps our greatest loss since the last century is simply a respect for the wonder of humanity and the existence of human life in the universe. Instead, the onward march of polarisation in life has led to a decline in our sense of community, of common unity and of the perfectly natural association between human beings. This is what its perpetrators most fear. To maintain dominion over the world, vast numbers of people must be weakened by being driven apart. A weakened population is a weakened world. The challenge before us is to *admit* this is happening to us, to seriously take action, and do all we can to reinstate a new, fully mature, common unity and solidarity. Surely, if we think about it, unity has to be nature's most treasured gift.

One factor that has contributed hugely to the loss of contact we have experienced with one another is automation. In today's society we no longer have people who serve us – instead we just tap cards and press buttons. I remember, years ago, the lovely man who filled my car with petrol, took my money and then brought back the change without me moving. He always chatted, and had the same friendly approach with all his customers. So much of what used to be real one-to-one contact with others has been lost.

Add to that the digital revolution, and we have been driven headlong into yet more isolation. Social media platforms were supposed to make us more connected, and at a very shallow, superficial level one could argue that they have. But at the same time, they seem to be doing a great job at separating, deepening divisions and keeping us physically apart from one another. Governments have so far totally failed to oversee and control some of social media's darker and more devastating effects on society. There is now such evil poison being transmitted through the airwaves, it's managing to actually kill people – even children.

Perhaps, though, the human population in the end will hold the trump card. Our species advancing not just in technology but in *self-knowledge* can become more mature in the realisation that human beings are much more deeply connected than they know – a reality too often obscured by circumstances and malevolent influences.

The notion of humanity's essential connectedness is no delusion, and is not grounded in sentimentality; it is simply a fact. One psychologist, Damian Hughes, describes it rather cleverly as an invisible social glue, only surfacing from time to time but never ceasing to amaze us. In that sense, it resembles a person willing to lose their own life while trying to save another from drowning. When asked why they did it, assuming they were lucky enough to survive, some cannot explain it. There are dozens of similar examples of our anonymous union with each other, all the time lodged within some deep part of us.

The implications are phenomenal. Unity may not require the effort we might think, because it is simply a natural part of who we really are. To return once again to Teilhard, he describes it as 'mutual internal affinity'. We may reject people, or not notice strangers. But even if ignored, that affinity is likely to emerge at any time, particularly in any sort of crisis. Think of wartime, when millions risk or even give up their lives to save others. In wartime, people become visibly connected and we get a glimpse of what a national effort can look like. Imagine this natural affinity between humans becoming fully acknowledged, exposed, forming a new unity and solidarity. Then look further ahead, and again, imagine a mutually interdependent *world society*. Most importantly, without any single country, or its population, losing one jot of their unique national identity. How vital it is in a crisis to try to see the bigger picture, and how much less daunting the future could be if the people were to unite.

It is more than possible. We *all* have this potential within us. To really discover and know the power of human connectedness, unity and solidarity, you have to enter into it, sign up to it and take an *active* part – which I will explore further on. Meanwhile, Timothy Snyder's words at the start of this chapter are a good place to begin in our daily lives. Seeing people through a different lens, and simply acknowledging others with any of those 'banal gestures'. Throughout the *Twenty Lessons*, Snyder inspires us and implores us to make eye contact with people, make small talk, join groups, make new friends, support charities and *involve* ourselves in any way we can in a united call for action.

I have to admit here to inadequacy in attempting to put into words the hidden dynamic of 'mutual internal affinity'. Not everything can be put into words – particularly something so potent, yet so hidden. However, thanks to someone I've never met, but who I have concluded is a genius, I have discovered a more direct, and much more powerful way to communicate it.

Karim Sulayman, a renowned classical musician, has made a brilliant three-minute film available on YouTube (see link on page 110). It is called *I Trust You*, and is recorded without drama, without a script, with no persuasive words, no acting and no manipulating. It uses one thing only: random, *ordinary people* in the street. If you watch it, you will see lucidly and clearly what I have struggled to say in words. And what I can promise is that you will then be left in no doubt. You may need a tissue handy. But what will also make you smile is a wonderful touch of irony – it was filmed outside Trump Tower!

8

Untold Hope

Living with lies and confusion on the surface can dull the flame of expectation, and what feels like impotence becomes normalised. Human energy sleeps and accepts nothing can be done. We shake our heads, fear for our future and our children and passively await the play of events.

Living with the truth turns all that on its head. Awakened energy leads to ambition, courage, daring and inspires a deep longing to do something to make a contribution to bring about change. We have to know we are better than the superficial chaos we are undergoing. Thousands of years of existence, of innovation, progress, the arts, culture, science and such massive achievements cannot be erased by such invasive malevolent influences. This should give us untold hope.

After Václav Havel

One person who has to stand out in history or in any political discussion, is Václav Havel, a man I can only refer to as a colossus. His small but profound book *The Power of the Powerless* is prefaced by an introduction from Timothy Snyder, who observes that 'The way to read *The Power of the Powerless* is to assume that it is right, and watch the world come into focus.' Havel fully comprehends what is wrong in the world. Yet in equal measure he understands the simplicity of how to put it right. What shines out in all his writing is his unshakeable belief in human life. There is only one thing that matters – *human existence*, which is central to everything.

Havel, a playwright and a poet, was a victim of the brutal Soviet regime that occupied Czechoslovakia in the last century. He was imprisoned for four years as a punishment after illegally publishing *The Power of the Powerless*, which has since become a much-acclaimed and timeless classic. He was an active dissident, imprisoned several times, but eventually went into politics himself and became president of his country. This gave him a wide grounding in politics as well as a deep insight into understanding how people become victims of totalitarian oppression. This oppression, he predicted, would in time grow to be even worse than the tyranny of the 1930s, and become what he called 'a complex, profound, and long-term violation of society'.

The unyielding passion that permeated all his writing, as with his contemporary Alexander Solzhenitsyn (see page 26) was that the aims of life and a thriving humanity come down to just one word: *truth*. Living with truth, instead of living a lie. What I most love about Havel is his ability to bypass unnecessary complexity and ascribe all the turmoil in society to simply living with a lie, instead of the truth. It's also astonishing that, in his gentle but strong and unyielding view, he was certain that if we could fully comprehend truth – particularly in relation to ourselves and our true human identity – we could change, or even more than that, *save the world*. Truth, he claims, has become lost to us, hidden away beneath the superficial surface of things, and untruth has become normalised.

My first full understanding of this was when I heard the following exchange on the TV news. 'Does the prime minister lie?' a voter was asked before an upcoming election.

'Yes,' came the reply.

'Will you still vote for him?'

'Definitely.'

That was a moment for me, a sudden realisation that lying is no longer a major issue in our contemporary world but is now perceived as normal and perfectly acceptable.

Havel saw all this coming but profoundly believed in the innate dignity and nobility of human beings, in which the truth could never be completely lost. For him, everyone has an 'inner sphere' in which the real aims of life, and an openness to truth, become eclipsed by lies and confusion. This is how he describes it: 'The flame of expectation is dulled, and what feels like impotence becomes normalised. Human energy sleeps and accepts nothing can be done.'

But, he assures us, something *can* be done. Being open to and 'living with the truth turns all that on its head'. Living with truth awakens energy, leads to ambition, courage and daring, and inspires a deep longing to do something, to make a contribution and to bring about change. 'We have to know we are better than the superficial chaos we are undergoing.' If I had to pick just one sentence to describe what Havel is trying to say, that would be it.

What to do? It begins with a willingness to be open to rediscovering the truth. Because we now live in a post-truth era, when we are enveloped daily in lies and untruth not just by the barons of partisan news media and dishonest politicians, but by the highly invasive social media platforms. Truth needs to make a comeback and needs the personal input of everyone.

As was said earlier, we sometimes don't know that we don't know. Yet we have to first *want* to know. Beneath the noise and clamour of everyday life, we can inadvertently bypass and neglect truth. Yet it remains the most precious of all human values.

For Havel, once truth is awakened, it can burst out. It can change our lives and our perspectives and enable us to experience the 'flame of expectation' by having discovered what he passionately calls 'the singular, explosive, incalculable, political power of living with the truth'. But there's more. Once the whole world understands the truth, then it's perfectly logical that, 'If the main pillar of the system is living a lie, then it is not surprising that the fundamental threat to it is living with truth.' How simple is that? Once humans understand their own invincible human power, the tyrants who rule by lies and deceit must surely lose their grip and ultimately fail.

Politics has to come from the people. Havel

wrote, 'If we want real and effective political power in our world, politics has to return to its only starting point – individual people who at present are enslaved by the modes and practices of untruth.' In a post-truth society, people are apathetic and demoralised, excluded from the structures of power, and no longer able to have any influence on those structures. For Havel, 'Exclusion is what lies at the root of all our present day moral and political misery.' Thus, by 'shedding the burden of traditional political categories', we are then free to open ourselves up to the real world of human existence.

Havel's prediction that oppression and tyranny would get worse turned out to be prophetic. Yet even he could not have envisaged the tsunami of lies and deception that is overwhelming us globally at this moment. This stems from the worst of those who wield power over us, of course, but alongside them (and serving their malevolence) is the aggressive advance of tech, media outlets and social media platforms now providing us with twenty-four-hour untruth. The problem is that serious, and getting ever harder to cope with.

Our values are being undermined, as is our national identity and our culture. We are the nation who joined forces and went to war to help another nation, gladly took in refugees and rescued children – a part of our caring culture and true identity. Think now of the scandals and disasters that have permeated public life in this country in recent years – from the Post Office scandal, in which postmasters faced wrongful conviction, to the PPE grifters of the Covid pandemic; from the lies of those who sold us Brexit, to the cynicism and xenophobia of far-right politicians today. These shameful episodes do not reflect the values of truth, fairness and justice on which our great national identity was built.

Everyone has the capacity to know what truth is, but we can be so preoccupied with the surface of things that it sometimes gets side-stepped. Perhaps one way of understanding its depth and value is considering how we feel when we're lied to, and how much it can hurt us. On a global scale, that is precisely what's happening, and the whole world is hurting. Havel wants us to go to war against untruth and, in unity, become the front line of a battle to reinstate truth and, in his words, 'turn untruth on its head'. To rediscover the truth of our existence, reignite the suppressed flame of expectation and awaken the energy that sleeps. We have to be aware of what truth is. And it starts with our everyday life – with the small, trivial truths we admit to ourselves as we go about our daily business – and in doing that we can reach a more profound truth about the bigger questions we face. Truth needs us all to make a commitment, a conscious effort to restore it at all levels, and then to know and be certain of the truth of human existence. This is a power that all other powers can only serve. If you quietly read the quote introducing this chapter over and over, you will discover that truth and, yes, 'untold hope', will be staring you in the face.

I want to add something here about the reality of hope. It comes from two ordinary people, like you and me, who have, in the gravest of circumstances, understood its truth.

The first is an amazing Israeli woman, Sharone Lifschitz, who lost her father in the hostage crisis in Gaza after the October 2023 Hamas attacks on Israel. It begins with Sharone's mother, who was kidnapped but later released from captivity. At the moment of her handover, in spite of her husband, at that time, still remaining captive, Sharone's mother reached out to her captors and bade them 'Shalom' wishing them peace.

Sharone was interviewed on the UK's Channel 4

News and commented on that overwhelming gesture, which she called 'impossible grace':

> Those who believe in the sanctity of life, and believe in each other as human beings, can look across the divide and offer a hand in peace and can see the pain in the other . . . What we now need is more understanding of each other's pain. There are many, many people that wish for peace and we have to be brave enough. If enough of us vie for peace, move towards peace, it will happen, it is in our hands.

Another astounding witness is bereaved mother Figen Murray, again speaking on Channel 4 News. Figen lost her son in the 2017 Manchester Arena bombing.

> When Martyn died, the amount of support, kindness, love and solidarity that poured out from the people of Manchester and from elsewhere was intense and massive. That really helped us as victims to cope with it. It's the kindness of others that made us able to carry on . . . We must absolutely as a society reject hate and any attempts to divide the nation.

It's just so important that we all see each other as one humankind and we need to exercise tolerance and compassion. We mustn't fear difference and we need to embrace difference as an enrichment to our lives.

9

The Future Is Us

> If humanity can see a new door opening above it, a new stage for its development; if each of us can believe that he or she is working so that the universe may be raised, in them and through them to a higher level – then a new spring of energy will well forth in the world's workers.
>
> Teilhard de Chardin, *The Future of Man*

Before I offer you some comments on the quotation above, I want to recall what initiated this project and where we started by offering you a brief metaphorical story.

Try to imagine some far-off aliens establishing an outpost in which they can observe planet Earth from outer space. At first glance they are overcome by its breathtaking beauty, and its majestic presence positioned in the vastness of space. They also marvel at how the sun is strategically positioned to support its existence. A tad nearer, and the earth would become a blazing inferno or a tad further away, a frozen wasteland. Just like the astronauts, they can actually see and marvel at its sheer awesomeness. Vast oceans, mountain ranges, great rivers, forests, lakes. Cities, towns, villages, architecture, and everywhere pulsating with every kind of unquantifiable life.

Then a much closer look reveals its tragedy beneath the beauty. A very small percentage of its human population who call themselves leaders are actively engaged in its destruction. Decimating rainforests, poisoning rivers and oceans, pumping large amounts of toxins into the atmosphere, which in turn are gradually destroying life that has survived over centuries. The climate collapse causing wildfires, floods and landslides. But that's only half of it. That very same small band of so-called rulers are creating destructive weapons. Waging wars and killing large swathes of the population. Their missiles and bombs obliterating whole families, wiping out entire villages, apartment blocks, hospitals, children in schools. Those who are not killed or maimed are becoming homeless, stateless refugees. Everything is being eroded: justice, human rights, values and culture. Watching on, the aliens recoil in horror. Convinced that unless some big change happens, our planet will not be able to sustain itself indefinitely. They return from where they came, stunned at the enormous destruction and sheer waste they have witnessed.

Meanwhile, back here on earth, it is not imagination that is needed but a long, cold look at reality. I refer you back to the Teilhard quote at the very beginning of the book: not only does it sum up everything I have attempted to communicate but also very simply gives us the answer. 'The human being can have no hope of an evolutionary future except in association with all the rest . . . and to not see it we would have to close our eyes.' James C. Scott puts it another way, echoing the idea of not seeing reality: 'Humanity's dark side blocks the light. Yet the light is there and nothing can extinguish it.' We are now forced to open our closed eyes, to see beyond the darkness that blocks us, and fully comprehend what is staring us in the face. As Teilhard says at the beginning of this chapter: 'If humanity can see a new door opening [and] a new stage for its development . . . a new spring of energy will well forth'. This is what I believe.

Perhaps I could revert back to my own personal story, which began in the introduction. It might explain how I arrived at this point. Since the 1960s, alongside my passion for good food, good wine and football, I have had a huge interest in the writings of Teilhard de Chardin and have read and studied as many of his books and essays as possible. He has had a huge influence on my thinking and affirmed for me another passion – my own belief in the essential goodness, and kindness, in human life.

Teilhard was a French Jesuit scientist who specialised in palaeontology, a branch of science concerned with the origins of life by the study of fossils, combining geology, biology and the study of evolutionary patterns. His seminal work was, for me, the book of all books on humanity, entitled very appropriately *The Human Phenomenon*. For me, the book uncovers the truth in its fullness. Human life really is a phenomenon. He was easily a century ahead of his time. His books and essays were banned by his Church and therefore not published in his own lifetime. Thankfully though, in 2003 an outstanding new translation of *The Human Phenomenon*, by Sarah Appleton-Weber, was published by Sussex Academic Press in England. Which itself is an amazing achievement; the former English translations did not really do him justice.

Teilhard saw the problems ahead that humans would be facing, but more importantly, he also saw the solutions. Over the years, particularly since the turn of the twenty-first century, I was sure his vision of humanity and its future was correct, but right now (hence the reasoning behind this book) that vision is becoming a reality. It involves, if I may put it this way, two phenomena: one, human beings are compelled to unite in order to survive. Two, when humans act in close unity, they discover their own person and who they really are, plus their own unique value, which then enables them to see all of that in others.

The quote at the start of the chapter is very simple but stands out as clear, shining truth. Once ordinary human beings fully understand the power of uniting and actually experience how this can unleash a 'spring of energy' they didn't know they had, they can then see a new door opening and a new form of human development. He says more. When humans unite they become an energy that all other energies can only serve. My own certainty comes from seeing Teilhard's vision beginning to be fulfilled. He not only perceived the necessity of humans uniting, but also, even more importantly, he knew it would be inevitable. As a scientist he saw the future of the whole world becoming convergent. So certain was he that he actually said it would be easier to stop the world from turning than to prevent convergence from happening.

Amazingly, contemporary scientists are indeed exploring a concept called convergent evolution. I am not an expert on this, but online explanations of the term break down the first word into its component parts: 'con' comes from the Latin for 'together', with 'verge' meaning 'turn towards'. The concept of 'convergence' in the modern scientific community entails a deeper integration of knowledge and an innovative approach focused on driving towards breakthroughs away from the laboratory, centred around real-world applications. All of this, too, in the name of solving societal problems. For those, unlike me, who have a scientific mind, there is a wonderful book called *Life's Solution* by Simon Conway Morris, a professor at Cambridge. This book is an empirical assessment of convergence in which he describes humans as now 'utterly different, we have new concerns, new priorities and questions, and most important of all, new possibilities'.

It's an approach that chimes perfectly with Teilhard's views. Another is from Yale Professor of Political Science Hélène Landemore, whose book *Politics Without Politicians* not only puts the case for new political systems very convincingly, but gives details of how a people's politics is now beginning to gather momentum with the advent of sortition and citizens' assemblies happening throughout the world.

Teilhard knew nothing of citizens' assemblies. Yet these assemblies are a manifestation of everything he expressed about what can be achieved when people unite on an equal footing, and how much more easily and swiftly society's problems might be solved. It is also so convincing for me, and so validating that other great minds within these pages have come to similar conclusions. In 2007 Nobel Laureate, then Secretary General of the United Nations, Kofi Annan wrote, 'I am convinced that Teilhard de Chardin is a thinker for the twenty-first century'.

What are we waiting for? The reasons behind my writing this book are chiefly because of my own anguish and refusal to accept what I now see is happening to our precious world. I am also totally sure there are millions more just like me who would do anything they could to bring about change. This is my hope.

If you have any doubts about envisaging just how a people's politics can be conceived, the answer is simple: all it needs is people. People in concert, as Hannah Arendt said, seeking how to constitute a 'stable worldly structure'. Obviously, seeking that structure is the first step, but it can only be conceived of by people at all levels of society, in all parts of the world, who want to come forward and offer their skills and talents as to how best to constitute that structure.

Change may be daunting, as is anything that at first seems impossible. But to give you an analogy – think of NASA, a united community of fired-up, enthusiastic people who just go on refusing to believe anything is impossible. NASA's ambition of one day taking humans to Mars must be overwhelmingly difficult. No oxygen, no water, and the infinite vacuum of space to overcome. But the scientists and engineers will not be deterred, because they are certain that if they pour enough hard work, ingenuity and energy into it, they will ultimately find a way! I have said this elsewhere, but human beings can, if they want to, achieve anything!

Let's end on that note of joy, and anticipation, because the good news is that all of this is actually beginning to happen. There is so much unseen, unknown kindness and goodwill everywhere, and away from all the noise and dissension, change is happening and the world is converging. There is not a lot we can do to stop it! There are many signs of hope and activity, assemblies, groups and associations. The world's workers are engaging in debate and shaping society around them. They are discovering Teilhard's new spring of energy and the real possibility of a new stage in our human development. We no longer have to be victims of tyranny and climate change but instead become masters of both. As a friend of mine said recently, 'revolution is already happening, we just haven't noticed it yet. The soil is ready; all we have to do is start planting'. Again, what are we waiting for? And by 'we', I mean you, me and eventually, I hope, all of us.

After all, the future is going to have to be Us.

> It is becoming evident that politics by no means need remain the affair of professionals, and that one simple electrician with his heart in the right place honouring something that transcends him and free of fear, can influence the history of his nation.
>
> Václav Havel,
> *The Power of the Powerless*

Afterword

Jamie Kelsey-Fry

I am one of the three people who founded the world's first Global Citizens' Assembly, which presented five times at the Glasgow COP climate conference in 2021. Since then, our team has established a global production house for the democracy renewal movement: One World or None (OWoN). We are sure that the only way to adequately address the climate crisis or the crisis of perpetual war for the last resources, is to deal with the fundamental crisis, which is in the way that humans come together to make decisions. Our operating systems need an upgrade.

The OWoN team has been involved in the development of deliberative and participatory democracy movements for decades. We have seen the power of Václav Havel's 'one simple electrician with his heart in the right place'. Those who find their agency through these processes, after a lifetime of being ignored, become an unstoppable force. They are who we have been waiting for. Not another political party, not another compelling ideology, not another charismatic leader . . . Just people like us. The regular people who are the fabric of everyday life. Our time has come.

Around 500 citizens' assemblies or citizens' juries have happened since the 1980s, 200 in the past five years. At a local level, national level and at a global level, regular citizens have been brought together by a democratic lottery-style system, have learned about an issue and deliberated together to reach a set of recommendations. The issues have ranged from refuse collection, healthcare and the environment to immigration, urban planning and electoral reform. They have consistently shown that regular people, once given all the information on any issue, invariably come up with common-sense and far-reaching solutions. They do this because they are free to. They do not have the constrictions of vested interests to appease, lobbyists to be swayed by, a career pole to climb, a political party line to stick to or an electorate to please. Václav Havel's 'one simple electrician' is free to act with common sense and the wellbeing of all as their sole concern.

In 2020 to 2021, I and two others convened a

loose group of organisations to co-create the world's first Global Citizens' Assembly. We eventually brought together 100 people from the entire human population, selected by a lottery-style system. The human family had never met itself before in this unique way: 70 per cent were living on $10 or less a day, 10 per cent had no formal education, 50 per cent were women and 13 per cent white. They met for 69 hours over 11 weeks, in 22 breakout rooms on Zoom, with translators, note takers and facilitators to support them. A goat herder from Socotra, a 19-year-old student from Wuhan, an elderly seamstress in Brasilia, a young farmer in the DR Congo and a social worker from Coventry. Whatever group you might have observed, you'd have come to the same conclusion . . . The default mode for humanity is compassion, a willingness to cooperate and a desire for our children to live in peace. At first, we were astonished at what great luck it was for us to have come across such examples of kindness and consideration of the highest order. And then we realised that is who we are, that is a human being, being human. When you put everything else aside and put us together and allow us to listen to each other, that is who we are. Our differences rapidly melt away and our commonality breaks through to the surface in the most extraordinary fashion. You wonder to yourself, 'how could I have forgotten this?'

The book you have just read captures the emergence of a global movement that has no name. A multiplicity of new ways by which humans come together to make decisions, is growing on every continent. In Africa, the young practitioners and facilitators we have worked with are convinced that this new system of making decisions is going to take off first there because everybody is so ready for this. A population that is so young is eager to adopt this upgrade in governance structures. But we have found that actually, wherever we go, everybody is ready for this. The research consistently shows that when people understand how these new systems work, with regular people chosen through a lottery-style system, between 60 per cent and 75 per cent of people would support these processes immediately.

Those interested in participating are not limited to the left of centre. The Sortition Foundation ran research in 2025 that showed that 69 per cent of Reform voters would support citizens' assemblies when they knew about them. In 2023 in Germany, research showed that the voting demographic most likely to support them when they heard about them were those drawn to the AfD. People are sick of feeling they have no agency, that their dignity has been stolen from them and that a lofty elite that rules over them has no care for their voice at all. It is hard to argue against these conclusions, of course, but a better answer than a move to the far-right may be to get behind these new participatory systems.

In 2007, the future European Commission President Jean-Claude Juncker said: 'We all know what to do, but we don't know how to get re-elected once we have done it.' The twenty-first century is confronting us with a multiplicity of crises that our systems are simply not built to address adequately. It is important to realise that if we are to get through these difficult times then we are going to have to get through them together. The difficult decisions that are going to have to be made will only really be accepted if we can see that it was regular, everyday people like us who were part of the decision-making process.

There is nothing more ordinary than upgrading an operating system when it is out of date. That is all that is happening here. Finally escaping the embarrassing polarisations of political party posturing and creaking ideologies that no longer fit the century that we are living through. The noble idea of democracy has long been denigrated by corruption, has been corporate captured and become the plaything of billionaires. This book allows us to remember that we are an extraordinary species capable of extraordinary things, and we haven't even started yet. All our genius and innovation as a species has been funnelled into increasingly efficient and cowardly ways to kill people, manufacturing increasingly absurd desires to consume increasingly vacuous rubbish and to keep a handful of men in positions of unheard-of power and privilege while turning people against each other in increasingly disturbing numbers. *We are better than this*. Delia's book is about humanity remembering itself, humanity restored. That is the key to this quiet revolution, so gracefully delivered in its pages. All that is needed now is for this story to get a lot louder.

Time for Action!

Our human species now stands on the threshold of a new age with the possibility of a great renewal of life on Earth. There are two options before us. Either a momentous universal joint effort to restore order to our dysfunctional world, or else we face the inevitable: the disastrous effects of climate change and the extinction of life on Earth as we know it.

On a personal note, in June 2026 Europe suffered the most extreme heat wave ever recorded. Suffolk, where I live, was the hottest place in England, with temperatures hitting 37.3°C. To experience that extreme heat and humidity felt as if there was no air to breathe, and for me became a stark reminder of what the future might be as our world gets hotter. Most frightening of all is not just knowing that it's going to get worse, but knowing that climate scientists are also predicting the effects of climate change will lead to a world-wide shortage of water. The consequences of which are unimaginable. Yet crucially what they are also predicting is that *if we act now*, we still have a chance of at least preventing the worst-case scenario. And doing that starts with all of us recognising our collective power to take ownership of our politics and our lives.

Is it now time for all of us to think more deeply about which direction we want to choose for the future? We can either choose to lose everything humanity has achieved throughout our history on Earth or we can start believing in truth. The truth of our existence which includes the dignity, nobility and true values of human life, alongside nature.

Can we not, at this juncture, try to start finally believing in ourselves, both individually and collectively? However advanced artificial intelligence becomes, and whatever robots can or can't do, ultimately those machines will be powerless to replace the intelligence of a conscious humanity. It will be down to us, and us alone, to undo the damage and poison of our incessant burning of fossil fuels, and to repair the devastation being dealt to our beautiful, life-sustaining planet.

Please can you help? Whoever you are, wherever you are, you are needed to join a far-reaching undertaking that will be like no other. No qualifications are needed – just the energy of each unique human being, willing to give what they have, to take a chance, to be brave, daring and impervious to criticism. But alongside that, something that overcomes all obstacles: the unmatched joy of closely sharing hardship and failure, as well as successes, with others. In combining our shared objectives and that sense of belonging to one another, we will draw out and reveal what Teilhard described as our 'mutual internal affinity'. It is that affinity that awaits its full recognition, and what will unite us in all our trials, struggles and uncertainties.

How can we make it happen? There is only one resource we need – people. No great leaders, only collaborative administrators. No elites, but everyone equal. No age barriers – we need the young and the old. Window cleaners and judges; aristocrats and barrow boys; the sick, the healthy, the housebound, the workers, the retirees. The economists, the bankers, the teachers, the nurses. All of these and more – and yes, those 'not at present in employment, education or training' (the Neets, as they are affectionately called). What we need is – everyone.

There is no precise blueprint as to how a people's politics might work – no rulebook, no instruction manual. It can only be devised by people willing to share their ideas, ingenuity and passion.

It will also need huge input from the arts – musicians, artists, writers, poets – not least to support and celebrate the bringing together of a whole world in this shared endeavour. And let's not forget that unity and solidarity, precious commodities though they are, cost nothing. How could any of us not want to be a part of that?

The future really is in our hands. Instead of waiting in the wings for disaster to happen, meekly accepting our fate, why can't we, the proud, united human species, simply step up, and at last become centre stage and masters of our own destiny, and our planet's future?

For more information visit Substack @TheUsProject

Acknowledgements

Nothing worthwhile is ever achieved by one person, so much gratitude goes to team Delia. Headed by Michael, my husband, the mainstay of everything I do. Alongside him, Ben, Lindsey and Melanie who should know how tremendously they have supported me throughout. So much gratitude also to Edmund Gould, my Editor, for his sensitive guidance and suggestions all through.

Another thank you goes to Maddy Price, Editorial Director at Canongate for her patience, comments and help, to Louise Tyler, Managing Editor, and Helen Bleck, Copy Editor, and to the whole Canongate team. A final thank you to Jamie Byng for his late-night reading of the original manuscript, and for then deciding to publish it.

Resources

If you want to explore some of the ideas I've discussed in *Us*, here are some suggested resources:

Hannah Arendt, *The Origins of Totalitarianism*. Penguin Modern Classics, 2017.

Hannah Arendt, *On Revolution*. Introduced by Jonathan Schell, Penguin Books, 1977.

Anne Applebaum, *Autocracy, Inc*. Allen Lane, Penguin Random House, 2024.

Richard J. Bernstein, *Why Read Hannah Arendt Now?* Polity Press, 2018.

Pierre Teilhard de Chardin, *The Future of Man*. Doubleday, 2004.

Pierre Teilhard de Chardin, *The Human Phenomenon*. Translated by Sarah Appleton-Weber, Sussex Academic Press, 2003.

James S. Fishkin, *Democracy: When the People Are Thinking*. Oxford University Press, 2020.

Václav Havel, *The Power of the Powerless*. Introduction by Timothy Snyder, Vintage Classics, Penguin Random House, 2018.

Brett Hennig, *The End of Politicians: Time for a Real Democracy*. Unbound, 2017.

Michiko Kakutani, *The Death of Truth*. William Collins, Harper Collins, 2018.

Michiko Kakutani, *The Great Wave*. William Collins, Harper Collins, 2024.

Peter Kropotkin, *Mutual Aid: A Factor in Evolution*. PM Press, 2018.

Hélène Landemore, *Politics Without Politicians – The Case for Citizen Rule*. Allen Lane, Penguin Random House, 2026.

James Miller, *Can Democracy Work?* Oneworld, 2020.

Moisés Naím, *The Revenge of Power*. Griffin, 2023.

James C. Scott, *Seeing Like a State*. Yale University Press, 2020.

James C. Scott, *Two Cheers for Anarchism*. Princeton University Press, 2012.

Delia Smith, *You Matter – The Human Solution*. Mensch, 2022.

Timothy Snyder, *On Tyranny: Twenty Lessons from the Twentieth Century*. Illustrated by Nora Krug, The Bodley Head, Penguin Random House, 2021.

Timothy Snyder, *The Road to Unfreedom: Russia, Europe, America*. Vintage, Penguin Random House, 2019 (also available in paperback).

Gary Stevenson, *The Trading Game*. Penguin Random House, 2025.

James Surowiecki, *The Wisdom of Crowds*. Abacus, 2004.

John Vaillant, *Fire Weather*. Sceptre, Hodder & Stoughton, 2023.

Online Resources

Carole Cadwalladr, *The Nerve*, thenerve.news

Carole Cadwalladr, *Facebook's role in Brexit – and the threat to democracy;* and *This Is What a Digital Coup Looks Like*, TED Talks, ted.com

Alastair Campbell and Rory Stewart, *The Rest Is Politics* podcast.

Alastair Campbell and Rory Stewart, *The Rest Is Politics: Leading* podcast.

Prime Minister Mark Carney, *Principled and pragmatic: Canada's path*, address to the World Economic Forum Annual Meeting, Davos, Switzerland, 20 January 2026, pm.gc.ca

Citizens' assemblies clips, allhandsondoc.com/films

Citizens' assemblies worldwide, buergerrat.de/en/citizens-assemblies/citizens-assemblies-worldwide

Citizens Reunited, citizensreunited.substack.com

Cumbria Climate Assembly, sharedfuturecic.org.uk

Brett Hennig, Sortition Foundation, *What if we replaced politicians with randomly selected people*, TED Talks, ted.com

Tom Holland and Dominic Sandbrook, *The Rest is History* podcast.

Julian Huxley and the Invention of the Public Scientist, Archive on 4, BBC Sounds, bbc.co.uk/sounds

Led by Donkeys, @LedbyDonkeys, www.youtube.com

Mr Nobody Against Putin, documentary directed by David Borenstein and Pavel Talankin, BBC, 2025, bbc.co.uk/iplayer

One World or None, Global Assembly film, oneworldornone.world

Orwell: 2 + 2 = 5, documentary directed by Raoul Peck, 2025, Amazon Prime Video or YouTube.

Pope Leo's Encyclicals: The Holy See, vatican.va

Rise of the Nazis, BBC, bbc.co.uk/iplayer

Anthony Scaramucci and Katty Kay, *The Rest Is Politics: US* podcast.

Gary Stevenson, *Garys Economics*, youtube.com/garys-economics

Timothy Snyder, *Thinking about . . .*, snyder.substack.com

Karim Sulayman, *Karim Sulayman – I trust you*, 19 November 2016, youtube.com

The National Conversation, www.thenationalconversation.org.uk

2073, docudrama directed and produced by Asif Kapadia, via Amazon Prime Video or YouTube.

Quote References

P.vii *'The human being can have . . .'*
Pierre Teilhard de Chardin, *The Human Phenomenon.* Translated by Sarah Appleton-Weber, Sussex Academic Press, 2003.

P.xi *'Democracy is a political system . . .'*
Elmer E. Schattschneider, *Two Hundred Million Americans in Search of a Government*, Holt, Rinehart & Winston, 1969.

P.9 *'When I was a child . . .'*
Paul's Letter to the Corinthians – 1 Cor. 13:11.

P.15 *'This is a stern invitation . . .'*
John Vaillant, *Fire Weather*. Sceptre, 2023.

P.17 *'You may drive out nature . . .'*
Horace, *Satires and Epistles* – 1.10.24. Translated by Christopher Smart, Harper & Brothers, 1853.

P.19 *'Beauty is truth, truth beauty . . .'*
John Keats, 'Ode on a Grecian Urn,' *Lamia*, *Isabella*, *The Eve of St. Agnes, and Other Poems*. Taylor and Hessey, 1820.

P.22 *'False and contrary to nature . . .'*
Pierre Teilhard de Chardin, *The Human Phenomenon.* Translated by Sarah Appleton-Weber. Sussex Academic Press, 2003.

P.26 *'The simple step of a . . .'*
Alexander Solzhenitsyn, *One Word of Truth . . . The Nobel Speech*. The Bodley Head, 1970.

P.27 *'We do not know what . . .'*

José Ortega y Gasset, *Man and Crisis*. Norton Library, 1962.

P.27 *'We look at this over . . .'*
Giles MacDonogh, *Rise of the Nazis*. BBC television series, produced by 72 Films, 2019.

P.29 *'The times we now live . . .'*
P.30 *' . . . strategy for gaining and . . .'*
P.30 *' . . . three Ps: Populism, Polarisation . . .'*
Moisés Naím, *The Revenge of Power*. Griffin, 2023.

P.32 *'Trump can lead the Western . . .'*
Alexei Pushkov, *Twitter* (now *X*), 13 February 2016.

P.39 *'Never has our future been . . .'*
Hannah Arendt, *The Origins of Totalitarianism*. Penguin Modern Classics, 2017.

P.43 *' . . . the vigour given to the . . .'*
P.44 *' . . . the representative organs could become . . .'*
Thomas Jefferson, letter to Samuel Kerchevel (1816), *The Works of Thomas Jefferson, Volume 12*. G.P. Putnam, 1904.

P.45 *'Nothing . . . can weed out the . . .'*
P.46 *' . . . we can speak of the . . .'*
P.46 *'Not only were many aspirations . . .'*
Peter Kropotkin, *Mutual Aid: A Factor in Evolution*. Heinemann, 1902.

P.47 *'Today, when there is . . .'*
Richard J. Bernstein, *Why Read Hannah Arendt Now?* Polity Press, 2018.

P.49 *'Yet I cannot too often . . .'*
Walt Whitman, *Democratic Vistas*. University of Virginia, 1871.

P.54 *'What Athens did have was community . . .'*
James Miller, *Can Democracy Work?* Farrar, Straus and Giroux, 2018.

P.59 *'The different branches of science . . .'*
Julian Huxley, introduction to *The Phenomenon of Man*. Pierre Teilhard de Chardin, Collins, 1959.

P.69 *'Tyrannical regimes arose at different . . .'*
Timothy Snyder, *On Tyranny: Twenty Lessons from the Twentieth Century*. Bodley Head, 2017.

P.72 *'There is greatness in each . . .'*
Abraham Maslow, *Motivation and Personality*. Pearson, 2007.

P.82 *'The flame of expectation is . . .'*

P.83 *' . . . the singular, explosive, incalculable, political . . .'*

P.83 *'If the main pillar of . . .'*

P.84 *'If we want real and . . .'*

'Exclusion is what lies at . . .'

Václav Havel, *The Power of the Powerless*, Vintage, 1978.

P.80 *'The way to read "The Power of the Powerless" . . .'*
Timothy Snyder's introduction to *The Power of the Powerless*. Václav Havel, Vintage, 2018.

P.87 *'Those who believe in the . . .'*
Sharone Lifschitz, Channel 4 News. 7 October 2025.

P.87 *'When Martyn died, the amount . . .'*
Figen Murray, Channel 4 News. 2 October 2025.

P.89 *'If humanity can see a . . .'*
Pierre Teilhard de Chardin, *The Future of Man*. Doubleday, 2004.

P.91 *'Humanity's dark side blocks the . . .'*
James C. Scott, *Seeing Like a State*. Yale University Press, 2020.

P.97 *'It is becoming evident that . . .'*
Václav Havel, *The Power of the Powerless*. Vintage, 1978.